The Galaxy of C
A Hilarious Space Adventure Where Everything (and Everyone) Could Go Wrong (Part 1)

Dr. Rabea Hadi

Board Certified Family Physician

Medical Scholar and Academic Trainer

Table of Contents:

Disclaimer 3
Your Free Gift 5
Why Should You Read This Book? 6
Introduction 8
Chapter 1: The Portal of All Mishaps 10
Chapter 2: Space Repairs (And Other Bad Ideas) 21
Chapter 3: The Great Escape (Sort of) 31
Chapter 4: The Social Dilemma 42
Chapter 5: The Space Diner Debacle 53
Chapter 6: Space Hitchhiker's Dilemma 65
Chapter 7: The Phobia Showdown 76
Chapter 8: The Curing Moment 87
More from the Author 99

Disclaimer

Information in this book is for education and entertainment purposes. For any mental, medical or financial advice, please consult a licensed professional. By reading this book, you agree that under no circumstances is the author responsible for any losses that are incurred due to using information within.

This is a work of fiction. Names, characters, places, and incidents either are products of the author's imagination or are used fictitiously. Any resemblance to actual persons, living or dead, events, or locales is coincidental.

Copyright © 2024 Dr. Rabea Hadi

All rights reserved.

No part of this book may be reproduced, stored in a retrieval system, or transmitted in any form or by any means, electronic, mechanical, photocopying, recording, or otherwise, without the prior written permission of the publisher and author, Dr. Rabea Hadi.

I appreciate your constructive feedback at

mail@chooseyourquest.net

Review at Amazon & Goodreads.

Your Free Gift

Dear Reader,

Thank you for your interest in my books! As a token of my gratitude, I'm thrilled to offer you selected parts from the first chapters of my other books, for free.

Scan here.

This book, like the one you're holding, is part of a series designed to boost mental health through engaging adventures.

While these books are not sequentially ordered and don't follow the same characters, each story provides valuable insights and tips for mental well-being.

If you enjoy my books, I would greatly appreciate your constructive review on Amazon and Goodreads. Also, visit my website https://chooseyourquest.net/ Your feedback helps other readers interested in mental health support and adventure discover these books.

Dr. Rabea Hadi

Why Should You Read This Book?

If you're looking for a hilarious, fast-paced space adventure filled with quirky characters, absurd encounters, and laugh-out-loud moments, *The Galaxy of Comedy* is the book for you! Whether you're a fan of witty banter, slapstick humor, or wild space hijinks, this book offers a refreshing and fun escape into the cosmos.

Here's why you'll love it:

- **Unique Characters with Relatable Fears**: Each crew member brings their own phobias and eccentricities, making for a cast that's both entertaining and surprisingly relatable. You'll laugh at their mishaps, cheer for their victories, and maybe even see a little of yourself in their struggles.
- **Non-Stop Comedy**: This isn't your typical sci-fi epic. It's a comedy-first adventure, mixing wordplay, puns, and absurd situations with thrilling space chases and dangerous encounters.

- **A New Kind of Adventure**: In the *Galaxy of Comedy*, anything can happen—and it usually does! From malfunctioning gadgets to intergalactic food fights, you'll be on the edge of your seat, wondering what chaos awaits around the next corner.
- **Feel-Good Escapism**: Sometimes, you just need a good laugh, and this book delivers. It's lighthearted, fun, and the perfect way to unwind while journeying through the stars.

If you enjoy clever, comedic twists on classic sci-fi adventures, then hop aboard the *Starduster* and join the crew as they navigate the wackiest galaxy you've ever seen!

Introduction

The galaxy is vast, mysterious, and filled with wonders beyond imagination. At least, that's what they tell you in every sci-fi movie. But for you, it's mostly a jumble of data sheets, lab reports, and making sure your boss doesn't nap through important meetings.

Your name isn't important right now—after all, you're just a lab assistant in the top-secret, multi-government intergalactic portal research project. *Super secret*, as Professor Otto likes to remind you. The kind of secret that everyone knows about but pretends they don't. The kind of secret that involves a lot of standing around and trying to look busy.

Professor Otto is a genius, no doubt about that. A brilliant mind, but with the organizational skills of a squirrel on coffee. Sleepy, sloppy, and more often than not, he forgets the very thing he's working on. But hey, that's where you come in.

Today, however, is not just any day. Today, you'll do more than clean up after Otto's coffee spills or shuffle papers. Today, you'll embark on a journey to a galaxy far beyond anything you've ever dreamed of. Or, at least, you'll stumble into it by accident.

You see, the portal Otto has been working on—a grand achievement that could change the course of history—isn't quite stable. And in a twist of events, you're about to find out just how unstable it really is.

Hold tight, because what's coming next is full of laughter, mishaps, and a crew of quirky characters who may or may not have any idea what they're doing. But hey, that's what makes it fun, right?

Welcome to the Galaxy of Comedy. Your journey is about to begin, and trust me—*everything* (and everyone) could go wrong.

Chapter 1: The Portal of All Mishaps

The lab is unusually quiet today, save for the soft snores of Professor Otto. He's curled up in his chair, head drooping onto a stack of notebooks, a thin line of drool connecting his cheek to a page filled with incomprehensible equations.

You sigh. It's your job to keep things in order, which usually means tidying up the professor's messes. But today, there's an air of anticipation. Otto's latest project—the intergalactic portal—stands gleaming in the center of the lab, wires and lights blinking in ways that suggest it's either about to work or explode. Knowing Otto, it's a 50/50 chance.

"Just another day in the lab," you mutter to yourself, picking up a mug with the words *World's Sleepiest Scientist* emblazoned on the side. Typical. Otto's not even awake to see the fruits of his labor.

As you turn to place the mug on the counter, something catches your eye. There, lying carelessly on the floor amidst a pile of notes, is the remote control to the portal activation device. The very device that Otto told you never to touch.

You bend down, picking it up gingerly, as though it might explode at any second. The device is surprisingly light for something so dangerous, with a bright red button in the center—cliché, right? But effective. Your instinct is to return it to the professor, but there's a nagging curiosity in the back of your mind. What could possibly go wrong?

Otto's snores grow louder. He's definitely not waking up anytime soon.

You hold the device in your hand, turning it over. It's just one button. How hard could it be?

Before you can stop yourself, your finger grazes the button. A soft click echoes through the lab, followed by a low hum as the portal begins to power up.

"Uh... Professor?" you call out, your voice rising with panic. "I think I... uh... might've turned on the portal?"

Otto remains blissfully unaware, still lost in whatever dreamland scientists drift to during their afternoon naps.

The hum grows louder. Lights flash across the lab, casting strange shadows on the walls. You back away slowly, hoping that maybe, just maybe, you can undo whatever it is you've done.

Too late.

The portal blinks to life with a sudden *whoosh*, sucking the air out of the room like someone opened a giant vacuum. You feel a tug at your feet, then at your entire body. Before you know it, you're being pulled toward the portal, the force growing stronger by the second.

"Professor Otto!" you scream, but the words are snatched away as you're yanked off the ground, the room spinning around you. Papers fly through the air, equipment clatters to the floor, and in the center of it all is you, spiraling toward the portal like a leaf caught in a whirlwind.

With a final, dizzying lurch, you're sucked into the glowing vortex.

Moments later...

You land face-first in something soft, squishy, and disturbingly jiggly. It smells faintly of blueberries.

Groaning, you push yourself up, trying to make sense of your surroundings. The lab is gone, replaced by a vast, purple-hued sky and a ground that seems to ripple beneath you like gelatin.

"Well, this isn't Earth," you mutter, brushing what appears to be glowing green dust off your clothes. You take a tentative step, only to bounce slightly off the gelatinous surface. Great. You're standing on an alien trampoline.

Before you can fully process the situation, a small, high-pitched voice calls out from behind you. "Ah! A newcomer! Welcome to the Bouncy Plains of Flubblor!"

You turn to find a creature that can only be described as… odd. It's roughly the size of a small dog but shaped like a lopsided cupcake, with far too many eyes and a body that wobbles with every step.

"Where am I?" you ask, still trying to get your bearings.

The creature beams—or at least you think it does, considering it doesn't exactly have a mouth. "You, my friend, are in the Galaxy of Comedy! Home of the funniest beings in the universe, where every day is a joke, and every joke could be your last!"

You blink. "What?"

"No time for questions! You've got to meet the others!" The creature starts bouncing off into the distance, its wobbly body jiggling with each leap. "Come on! Before the sky starts telling knock-knock jokes again!"

You sigh, but there's really no other option. Reluctantly, you follow the bouncing creature, trying not to trip over your own feet as the ground continues to ripple beneath you.

Welcome to the Galaxy of Comedy, indeed.

You follow the bouncing cupcake-shaped creature across the gelatinous plains, your feet sinking into the squishy ground with every step. Each time you try to walk faster, the surface beneath you wobbles, making it feel like you're walking on a giant bowl of Jello. Not exactly the easiest terrain for a graceful exit.

The cupcake-creature hops ahead, its strange body wobbling so wildly that you're half-expecting it to topple over. "Hurry up! The others are waiting, and the last thing we need is for the sky to start its stand-up routine again."

"The sky... what?" you mutter, trying to keep up, but you don't have time to ask more questions.

Ahead of you looms a strange structure—a towering spire made of what looks like interwoven noodles, glowing in different shades of blue and green. The creature skids to a halt in front of the entrance, bouncing slightly as it comes to rest.

"You first!" it chirps, gesturing toward the spire with what you assume is some form of limb.

You hesitate, peering up at the spire. "Is this safe?"

The creature tilts what could only be its head, though it's hard to tell given its bizarre anatomy. "Safe? No! This is the Galaxy of Comedy! We're all about fun, not safety!"

You sigh. Of course. Safety is overrated, right?

With no other choice, you step forward and approach the noodle spire, your feet sinking slightly into the gelatinous ground as you go. Just as you're about to reach the entrance, the creature hops in front of you, blocking your way.

"Wait, wait, wait! Before you go in, I have to warn you about the others," it says, its voice suddenly serious—or as serious as something that looks like a sentient cupcake can sound.

"The others?" you ask, raising an eyebrow.

"Yes, yes," it says, bobbing slightly. "You'll see them soon enough. They're... well, they're unique. You'll like them, I'm sure, but be prepared. Not everyone here is, shall we say, *stable*."

Great. More unstable people to deal with. Just what you needed. You nod, motioning for the creature to move aside. "Got it. I'll be prepared."

The creature giggles and hops away, giving you room to finally enter the spire. You take a deep breath and step inside.

Inside, the noodle spire is even more bizarre than it looked from the outside. The walls pulse with glowing light, and the floor beneath your feet feels oddly sticky. It's as though you've stepped into a giant bowl of spaghetti, but with less sauce and more weirdness.

Ahead of you, a small group of figures huddles around what looks like a makeshift control panel. You can hear voices, though their conversation is too muffled to make out. You take a few steps closer, trying to get a better look.

"Hello?" you call out.

The group turns toward you, and your heart skips a beat when you recognize one of the figures.

It's **Matilda**, one of the senior scientists from the lab. She's the last person you expected to see here—prim, proper, and always in control. Except now, she's standing on what appears to be a floating platform, several feet off the ground, and she looks absolutely *terrified*.

"Matilda?" you ask, shocked. "What are you doing here?"

Matilda's face is pale, her knuckles white as she grips the edge of the floating platform. "What am I doing here? What are *you* doing here?! Get me down from this ridiculous contraption!"

You glance up at her, trying to figure out how she even got onto the platform in the first place. "Are you... stuck?"

Matilda's eyes widen, and for a moment, she looks like she's about to faint. "Of course I'm stuck! And if I move an inch, I'll plummet to my death!"

You blink, looking at the platform, which is maybe ten feet off the ground at best. "I'm not sure you'll die, Matilda. Maybe a sprained ankle at worst."

"That's not the point!" Matilda snaps, her voice rising an octave. "I have a *phobia of heights*, and I refuse to move from this platform until someone gets me down safely."

You pinch the bridge of your nose, already feeling the headache coming on. Matilda is always so composed and in control, but you've seen this side of her before—the side that absolutely freaks out when anything involves heights. And right now, she's clearly in full freak-out mode.

"Okay, okay, calm down," you say, trying to soothe her. "I'll figure something out. Just... stay still."

"Not a problem!" Matilda squeaks, clinging to the platform like a cat stuck in a tree.

You glance around, searching for a way to get her down without making things worse. The noodle walls pulse gently, casting a strange glow over the room. There has to be something you can use—anything to get Matilda off that platform without triggering a full-blown panic attack.

As you search, you hear another voice—a familiar, gruff voice that instantly makes you roll your eyes.

"Matilda! Quit making a fuss, would ya? You're fine up there," comes the voice of **Grump**, the crew's engineer, who's tinkering with a strange-looking gadget in the corner. He barely glances up from his work, waving one hand dismissively.

Grump is as eccentric as they come—brilliant when it comes to machines, but completely out of touch with human emotions. He's got a knack for fixing things, but he also has a tendency to make every situation worse with his *experimental* gadgets.

"You don't understand, Grump!" Matilda shouts, her voice shaking. "I'm not coming down until someone—*anyone*—rescues me from this nightmare!"

Grump sighs, finally looking up from his contraption. "Fine, fine. Hold on a sec."

Before you can object, Grump pulls out a device from his toolkit that looks suspiciously like a toaster with extra wires sticking out. "Here, this should do the trick." You stare at the device, a sinking feeling in your stomach. "Grump… what is that?"

Grump grins. "It's a portable gravity manipulator! I've been working on it for weeks. Just flip this switch, and Matilda will float gently to the ground."

"Are you sure that's safe?" you ask, eyeing the device warily.

"Safe? Pfft. Nothing's *safe* in space, kid," Grump says, flipping the switch without a second thought.

The device lets out a loud *pop* and a cloud of smoke. For a moment, everything goes still. And then Matilda begins to rise.

"Grump!" Matilda shrieks as the platform shoots upward, carrying her with it. "This is the *opposite* of what I wanted!"

You groan, watching as Matilda floats higher and higher, her panic growing by the second. Grump scratches his head, clearly perplexed. "Huh. Must've wired it backward." "Fix it!" you shout, glaring at Grump as you run to try to figure out how to stop the floating platform.

Chapter 2: Space Repairs (And Other Bad Ideas)

Matilda's shriek is still echoing in your ears as you stare up at her, floating higher and higher on the out-of-control platform. For a woman who always claims to be in charge of her emotions, she's currently clinging to the edge of the floating structure like a cat to a ceiling fan.

"Grump!" you shout again, hoping he'll realize the gravity—pun intended—of the situation. But Grump is still fiddling with his makeshift device, as calm as ever, clearly enjoying the challenge.

"Relax, kid," Grump says with a dismissive wave. "I just need to reverse the polarity or something science-y like that."

"Something *science-y*?" You can't help but feel a bit panicked. "Can you fix this before Matilda starts orbiting the spire?"

Grump snorts. "Please. I've got this."

Meanwhile, Matilda is still floating upwards, her eyes wide with terror. "I'm not okay with this! This is definitely *not* okay!"

You glance around frantically, trying to think of a solution that doesn't involve Grump's wild experiments. The glowing noodle walls seem to shimmer in mockery, casting strange shadows on the floor. But then your eyes land on the control panel, and you wonder if there's a way to bring Matilda back down without further catastrophe.

Ignoring Grump's increasingly erratic tinkering, you dash over to the control panel. The buttons and switches look unfamiliar, covered in alien symbols that could mean anything from "activate" to "self-destruct." Still, it's worth a shot.

"What are you doing?" Grump asks, finally noticing your actions.

"Fixing this before Matilda becomes a permanent part of the ceiling décor," you reply.

You hesitate for a moment, fingers hovering over the controls. Then, with a deep breath, you press the largest button, hoping for the best.

There's a brief pause. Then a loud, ominous *click*.

For a second, nothing happens, and you almost feel relieved. But then you hear a soft *whirr*, followed by Matilda's scream getting louder.

You look up just in time to see the platform begin its descent—at breakneck speed.

"Oh no, oh no, oh no!" Matilda screeches, gripping the platform for dear life.

"Grump!" you yell, panic setting in. "I think I made it worse!"

Grump raises an eyebrow. "Worse? That's subjective."

Before you can respond, the platform hits the ground with a bone-jarring *thud*. Matilda lets out a final shriek as she tumbles off the platform and lands in a heap on the squishy floor. You rush over to help her up, trying to suppress a laugh as she glares at you through her tangled hair.

"Never again," she hisses, brushing off her lab coat. "I am never *ever* getting on one of those floating death traps again."

"Well, technically, it's not a death trap if you survive," Grump says casually, still fiddling with his device. "You're welcome, by the way."

Matilda shoots him a withering glare, and for a second, you're sure she's going to strangle him. But instead, she simply straightens her coat, composes herself, and says, "This is why I despise space travel."

You help Matilda stand, trying to suppress your own nerves. "Let's just focus on figuring out where we are and how we can get back to the lab before any more floating platforms show up."

Grump looks up from his gadget, squinting at the walls of the spire. "Yeah, about that... I don't think we're in Kannas anymore, Ta da."

"Was that a reference to *something*?" you ask, bewildered. "Where did you even—"

But before you can finish, a strange noise interrupts you. It's a low rumble, almost like the sound of a distant engine... except it seems to be coming from the ground beneath your feet. You freeze, exchanging worried glances with Matilda and Grump.

"What was that?" Matilda whispers, her voice tight with anxiety.

Grump taps the ground with his boot, listening intently. "Sounds like something's coming. I'd say it's either a malfunctioning power core or something alive."

"Something alive?" you repeat, dread creeping into your voice. "That's not exactly comforting."

As if on cue, the rumbling grows louder, and the gelatinous floor beneath you begins to tremble.

You take a step back, your heart racing, as the walls of the spire start to vibrate.

Matilda clutches your arm. "We need to get out of here."

"Agreed," you say, glancing around for an exit. But before any of you can move, the floor suddenly splits open with a loud crack, revealing a dark, cavernous hole beneath your feet.

For a split second, you're suspended in midair, staring down into the abyss.

And then the floor gives way completely, and all three of you are sent tumbling into the darkness.

The Drop

The fall seems to last forever, your body weightless as you plummet through the dark void. You can hear Grump shouting something behind you, but the wind rushing past your ears drowns out his words. Matilda's panicked gasps echo in the darkness, and you instinctively reach out, grabbing onto something—anything—to stop your descent.

Finally, with a sickening thud, you hit the ground. It's soft, at least—much like the gelatinous plains you were walking on earlier. You groan, rolling onto your back and staring up at the hole you just fell through. It seems impossibly far above now, a tiny pinprick of light in the distance.

"Ow," you mutter, rubbing your sore limbs.

Grump lands next to you with a loud grunt, followed shortly by Matilda, who lands in a heap beside you, once again looking as though she's reconsidering every life choice that led her to this point.

"I am *never* traveling through space again," Matilda declares, her voice shaking with fury. "First floating platforms, now endless pits? This is absurd."

"Yeah, well, welcome to the Galaxy of Comedy," Grump says, standing and dusting himself off. "Absurd is kind of the theme here."

You look around, trying to get your bearings. The darkness of the cavern makes it hard to see anything, but the faint glow from the walls above illuminates enough to reveal that you've landed in what looks like a massive underground chamber. Strange, pulsing lights flicker from the walls, casting eerie shadows across the room.

"Well," you say, getting to your feet, "at least we didn't land on anything dangerous."

"Yet," Grump adds helpfully, pulling a flashlight from his toolkit. He switches it on, casting a narrow beam of light across the chamber. "Let's see where we ended up."

The three of you start walking cautiously, the soft squelch of your footsteps the only sound in the cavern. The ground beneath your feet feels slightly sticky, like the surface of a half-set gelatin mold, and every step sends a ripple through the strange substance.

"I have a bad feeling about this," Matilda mutters under her breath, glancing nervously at the walls. "What if there's something down here with us?"

Grump chuckles. "Well, if there is, it hasn't tried to eat us yet. That's a good sign."

"Not helpful," Matilda snaps, her eyes darting around as if expecting something to leap out at any moment.

You're about to tell her to calm down when something catches your eye. Up ahead, barely visible in the dim light, is a large, shadowy figure. It's hard to make out, but it seems to be moving—slowly, methodically, like it's pacing back and forth.

You stop in your tracks, holding up a hand to signal the others. "Wait... do you see that?"

Grump raises his flashlight, pointing it toward the figure. The light cuts through the darkness, illuminating what appears to be a massive, robotic creature. It's humanoid in shape but easily twice your height, with thick, mechanical limbs and a head that resembles a sleek, metallic helmet.

The creature pauses, turning toward the light, and you feel a shiver run down your spine as its glowing red eyes lock onto yours.

"Oh, great," you whisper, taking a step back. "Now what?"

The robotic figure takes a slow, deliberate step forward, its footsteps echoing through the chamber. You can see its joints creaking as it moves, and for a brief moment, you wonder if it's friendly… or if it's about to turn you into space dust.

Grump, ever the optimist, grins and steps forward. "Relax, I've dealt with these things before. Just let me handle it."

Matilda and you exchange nervous glances as Grump approaches the robot, his arms spread wide in what you assume is a gesture of peace.

"Hey there, big guy!" Grump calls out, his voice cheerful. "We're just passing through. No need to get all aggressive, alright?"

The robot doesn't respond. Instead, it raises one of its massive arms, a low whirring sound filling the air as its joints shift into position.

Grump's smile falters slightly. "Uh... maybe we could talk about this?"

Before anyone can react, the robot's arm swings down, narrowly missing Grump by inches. The force of the blow sends a gust of wind rushing past you, and Grump dives to the side just in time.

"Okay, not friendly!" Grump yells, scrambling to his feet. "Definitely not friendly!"

Matilda grabs your arm, pulling you back. "We need to get out of here. Now!"

You don't argue. With the robot now fully activated and clearly not in the mood for conversation, the three of you turn and sprint across the cavern, your feet slapping against the sticky ground as you run for your lives.

Chapter 3: The Great Escape (Sort of)

The sound of the robot's footsteps reverberates through the cavern, each thundering step shaking the ground beneath your feet. You run faster, dodging glowing rocks and sticky patches of gelatinous goo that threaten to trip you up. Grump's heavy breathing comes from behind, while Matilda—despite her usual composure—lets out panicked grunts every time she stumbles.

"Do you have any idea where we're going?" Matilda yells, her voice strained.

"Not a clue!" you shout back, glancing over your shoulder. The robot is still in pursuit, its glowing red eyes locked onto your group with laser focus. It's gaining ground, its metal limbs clanging with mechanical precision.

Grump, true to form, doesn't seem nearly as concerned as he should be. "Hey, if we get caught, maybe it just wants to ask us some questions! Maybe it's misunderstood!"

"Misunderstood?" Matilda snaps, barely dodging a jagged rock jutting out of the ground. "It's trying to flatten us like pancakes!"

Grump huffs as he jogs next to you. "Maybe that's its way of saying hello."

"Not the time for jokes, Grump!" you say, feeling your lungs burn as you try to keep pace.

The cavern seems to stretch on forever, with no clear exit in sight. Your mind races, trying to figure out how you're going to escape this situation alive—and in one piece. The robot's footsteps grow louder, and you know you're running out of time.

And then you see it: up ahead, faintly illuminated by the glowing walls, is what looks like an archway. It's low and narrow, barely big enough for a person to squeeze through, but it might just be your way out.

"There!" you shout, pointing to the archway. "Head for that opening!"

Matilda spots it too, and her eyes widen with a mixture of hope and desperation. "Are you sure it's not a dead end?"

"No, but we're about to find out!" you reply, not slowing down for a second.

The three of you dash toward the archway, your feet slapping against the sticky ground. As you approach, you realize the archway is even narrower than it looked—barely wide enough for a person to fit through, let alone a giant robot.

Matilda reaches the archway first, and without hesitating, she squeezes herself through. "Hurry!" she calls back.

You're next, ducking your head as you shimmy through the tight opening. It's a bit of a squeeze, but you manage to pop through on the other side. Grump, on the other hand, isn't as lucky.

He's halfway through when the robot catches up.

The sound of clanging metal and whirring gears fills the air as the robot swings one of its massive arms toward Grump. You can hear the whoosh as the arm sails through the air, narrowly missing his legs.

Grump struggles to squeeze the rest of the way through, grumbling under his breath. "It's not my fault this stupid hole is so small! Just give me a sec—"

Another metal arm swings down, and this time it hits the archway, smashing a chunk of rock loose. You can feel the ground shake beneath your feet as the robot slams against the wall, determined to break through.

"Grump, move it!" you shout, grabbing his arm and yanking with all your strength.

With one final tug, Grump is pulled through the archway, and the three of you stumble backward, falling into a heap on the other side. The robot's glowing red eyes peer through the narrow opening, but it's too big to follow.

For a moment, there's only silence, save for the heavy breathing of your group and the occasional clanking of the robot's limbs as it tries—unsuccessfully—to squeeze through the archway. It bangs against the stone wall a few more times before finally giving up, its glowing eyes fading into the darkness.

Matilda lies on the ground, panting. "I swear... this is the worst... trip... of my life."

Grump, ever the optimist, grins as he picks himself up. "Could've been worse! At least we're not robot pancakes."

You roll your eyes, getting to your feet. "Let's just be thankful we made it out in one piece."

Matilda sits up, brushing dirt from her clothes. "I don't suppose you have a plan for what happens next?"

You glance around the new chamber you've found yourselves in. The archway led to a much smaller space, dimly lit by the same glowing lights that lined the walls of the previous cavern. There's no sign of the robot following you, but there's also no obvious way out.

"We need to keep moving," you say, taking a cautious step forward. "There's got to be an exit somewhere."

"Or maybe there's a treasure hidden in here," Grump suggests, still tinkering with his gadgets. "Ancient alien tech, maybe? Something cool?"

Matilda groans. "I'd settle for a spaceship. Or a nice, solid ground that doesn't squish under my feet."

The three of you begin to explore the chamber, scanning the walls for any sign of an exit. The glowing lights pulse rhythmically, casting strange shadows on the floor, but there's no immediate indication of where to go.

As you move deeper into the chamber, something strange catches your eye—a small, metallic object wedged between two rocks on the far side of the room. It's about the size of a toaster, with blinking lights and a series of buttons on the side.

"What's that?" you ask, moving closer to inspect it.

Grump's eyes light up when he sees it. "Oh, now we're talking!" He rushes over, pushing past you to get a closer look. "This has got to be some kind of alien tech. Look at the design! The craftsmanship! I bet this thing could teleport us out of here in an instant!"

Matilda crosses her arms, looking skeptical. "Or it could vaporize us on the spot."

"Only one way to find out," Grump says, grinning as he presses one of the buttons on the device.

You and Matilda both take a step back, bracing yourselves for the worst. But instead of an explosion or sudden disintegration, the device lets out a soft *beep*, and the blinking lights begin to glow brighter.

Grump's grin widens. "See? Nothing to worry about! Now let's see what this baby can really do."

Before you can stop him, Grump presses another button, and the device emits a low hum. The ground beneath your feet trembles slightly, and for a brief moment, you wonder if Grump was actually right this time—maybe this is some kind of teleportation device, and you're about to be whisked away to safety.

But then, the humming grows louder, and the lights on the device start to flicker erratically. Grump frowns, tapping the side of the device as if that will fix it.

"That doesn't sound good," you say, taking another step back.

Grump shrugs. "It's probably just warming up."

"Or malfunctioning," Matilda mutters, edging away from the device.

Suddenly, with a loud *pop*, the device emits a blinding flash of light, and the room is filled with thick, billowing smoke.

You cough, waving your hand in front of your face to clear the air. "Grump, what did you do?"

Grump, for once, looks a little sheepish. "Uh... maybe I pressed the wrong button."

"Maybe?" Matilda snaps, glaring at him through the smoke. "You nearly blew us up!"

The smoke begins to clear, and as the haze lifts, you notice something strange. The walls of the chamber seem... different. The once smooth, glowing surfaces have been replaced by jagged, uneven rocks, and the floor beneath your feet is now solid stone.

"Wait a second," you say, looking around in confusion. "Where are we?"

Grump scratches his head, frowning. "Huh. Looks like we got transported somewhere after all."

Matilda steps forward, her eyes narrowing as she takes in the new surroundings. "This doesn't look like the same cavern."

You move closer to the center of the room, still trying to make sense of what just happened. The device that Grump activated lies on the floor, now smoking and sparking slightly, its blinking lights completely dead.

"Great," you mutter. "Now we're stuck in a completely different cave."

Grump, however, doesn't seem the least bit bothered. "Hey, it could be worse! At least we're not being chased by a giant robot anymore."

Matilda looks like she's about to argue, but before she can, something catches her eye. She points to the far side of the chamber, where a narrow tunnel leads out of the room.

"Look," she says, her voice cautious. "There's a way out."

You glance toward the tunnel, feeling a mix of relief and apprehension. It's not exactly the grand exit you were hoping for, but at this point, any escape route is better than none.

"Well, we're not going to find out by standing here," you say, motioning for the others to follow. "Let's see where this tunnel leads."

Matilda and Grump exchange a glance, then nod in agreement. Together, the three of you make your way toward the tunnel, hoping that this time, you'll actually find a way out of this crazy place.

The Tunnel

The tunnel is long and narrow, barely wide enough for the three of you to walk side by side. The air is cooler here, and the walls are rough and uneven, making it difficult to see where you're going.

Grump takes the lead, his flashlight illuminating the way ahead. "This is exciting, isn't it? Who knows what kind of alien wonders we'll find down here?"

Matilda rolls her eyes. "I'll settle for a door that leads back to the lab."

You chuckle softly, but deep down, you're just as anxious as Matilda. The Galaxy of Comedy has proven to be anything but predictable, and you have no idea what awaits you at the end of this tunnel.

As you continue walking, the tunnel begins to slope downward, and the air grows even colder. The walls close in around you, making you feel like you're descending into the depths of some ancient underground labyrinth.

Finally, after what feels like hours of walking, you reach the end of the tunnel. It opens into a large, open cavern, much like the ones you've already explored—but this one is different.

In the center of the cavern stands a massive, glowing structure. It's unlike anything you've ever seen before, with intricate patterns and symbols etched into its surface. The light it emits is soft and pulsating, casting an ethereal glow across the entire chamber.

Grump lets out a low whistle. "Now *that's* what I'm talking about."

Matilda's eyes widen in awe. "What... is it?"

You step forward, your gaze fixed on the glowing structure. It looks like some kind of ancient alien artifact, but its purpose is unclear. Could this be your way out? Or is it just another trap, waiting to spring?

Only one way to find out.

Chapter 4: The Social Dilemma

You stand at the entrance of the cavern, staring at the massive, glowing structure in the center. It towers over you, pulsing with an eerie, yet oddly calming, light. The patterns etched into its surface seem to shift and move as though alive, drawing your gaze into a hypnotic rhythm. It's unlike anything you've ever seen before, and for a brief moment, you wonder if it's the key to getting back home.

Grump, ever the curious engineer, steps forward first. His eyes are wide with excitement, like a kid on Christmas morning. "This… this is incredible! Do you know how valuable this kind of alien tech is? I bet I could reverse-engineer this thing and make a fortune."

Matilda, standing a few feet behind, crosses her arms and raises an eyebrow. "Or you could blow us all up. Again."

Grump waves her off, his attention fully locked on the glowing artifact. "Pfft. No way. This thing is a goldmine of advanced technology! We're talking years—no, decades—beyond anything we've got back at the lab."

You can't help but feel a twinge of unease as you watch Grump approach the structure. His overconfidence has already caused enough problems today, and you're not sure you want to see what happens if he starts messing with an alien artifact that you don't fully understand.

"Grump, maybe we should—" you begin, but you're interrupted by a soft, melodic humming sound that seems to come from the artifact itself.

The three of you freeze, listening intently as the hum grows louder. It's not mechanical, like the whirring of the robot from earlier—it's something… alive. The sound sends a shiver down your spine.

Matilda takes a cautious step back. "That's not normal."

"No kidding," you mutter.

The humming continues to build, filling the cavern with a strange, otherworldly resonance. And then, suddenly, the air in front of the artifact shimmers, and a figure begins to materialize out of thin air.

At first, it's just a faint outline, barely visible. But within seconds, the figure solidifies, standing tall and imposing in front of the glowing structure. It's humanoid in shape, but its skin is a soft, translucent blue, and its eyes glow with the same light as the artifact behind it.

The three of you stare in stunned silence as the figure opens its mouth to speak.

"Greetings," it says in a voice that's simultaneously calm and commanding. "I am Zenith, the Keeper of the Nexus. You have trespassed upon sacred ground."

Grump, ever the optimist, takes a step forward. "Trespassing? No, no! We're just... admiring your beautiful artifact here. Didn't mean to intrude!"

Zenith's glowing eyes narrow slightly. "This Nexus is not for admiration. It is a gateway to the Great Consciousness, a link between the minds of all those who enter its domain."

Matilda gives you a sideways glance. "That doesn't sound good."

You take a step forward, raising your hands in a placating gesture. "Look, we didn't mean to trespass. We're just... a little lost. We accidentally activated a portal and ended up here. We're trying to find our way home."

Zenith tilts its head, studying you carefully. "Lost, you say?"

"Very," you reply, doing your best to keep your voice steady. "We're not here to cause trouble. We just need help getting back to our own galaxy."

The figure's expression doesn't change, but it seems to consider your words for a moment. Then, slowly, it raises a hand and points toward the glowing artifact behind it.

"The Nexus can guide you to your destination," Zenith says. "But only if you are worthy."

Matilda lets out a soft groan. "I knew there'd be a catch."

Grump, of course, is already looking excited again. "Worthy, huh? I'm sure we're plenty worthy! What do we have to do? Answer some riddles? Solve a puzzle? I love this kind of stuff!"

You, on the other hand, are less enthusiastic. "Let's not get ahead of ourselves, Grump."

Zenith's glowing eyes seem to bore into you as it continues. "The Great Consciousness is a collective of minds from across the galaxy. To pass through the Nexus, you must open yourselves to it—allow it to connect with your thoughts, your fears, your desires."

Matilda stiffens visibly. "I don't like where this is going."

"Neither do I," you mutter, but there's not much choice at this point. You need to get back home, and if this Nexus is your only way out, you're going to have to play along.

Grump, naturally, steps forward first. "All right! Let's do this! Connect me to the Great Consciousness or whatever. I'm ready!"

Zenith turns its gaze to Grump, and for a moment, the air around him shimmers. Grump's expression changes slightly, his usual confidence faltering as a strange, distant look crosses his face.

You watch, nervous, as Zenith speaks again. "The Great Consciousness requires that you confront your deepest fear."

Grump's eyes widen. "My deepest fear? Ha! That's easy. Nothing scares me!"

Zenith raises a hand, and the shimmering light intensifies. "We shall see."

For a moment, nothing happens. Then, without warning, a loud buzzing sound fills the air, and a massive swarm of bees materializes out of thin air, swirling around Grump in a chaotic cloud.

Grump lets out a yelp of terror, his hands flailing wildly as he tries to swat the bees away. "Bees? Why is it always bees?!"

You stare in disbelief. "Bees are your greatest fear?"

Grump continues to panic, swatting at the bees as they buzz around his head. "You don't understand! I had a bad experience with a beehive when I was a kid!"

You can't help but chuckle as you watch Grump's uncharacteristic display of fear. The once-confident engineer is reduced to a flailing, terrified mess, all because of a swarm of holographic bees.

Zenith watches calmly as the scene unfolds. "Only by confronting your fear can you pass through the Nexus."

Grump, still swatting at the bees, glances at Zenith with wide eyes. "How do I make them go away?"

"By accepting them," Zenith replies.

"Accept them? They're bees!" Grump shouts, his voice cracking. "You don't just *accept* bees!"

You and Matilda exchange amused glances as Grump continues to flail about, but after a few more moments of swatting and shouting, something changes. Grump stops moving, standing perfectly still as the bees continue to buzz around him.

You hold your breath, waiting to see what happens next.

Grump closes his eyes, taking a deep breath. "Okay... okay... they're just bees. They're not real. They're not going to hurt me."

As soon as the words leave his mouth, the bees begin to fade, their buzzing growing softer and softer until it disappears altogether. The air clears, and the holographic bees vanish, leaving Grump standing alone in the center of the room.

Zenith nods approvingly. "You have faced your fear. You may proceed."

Grump lets out a shaky laugh, wiping sweat from his forehead. "Whew! That was intense! But hey, I did it!"

Matilda arches an eyebrow. "You were afraid of *bees*?"

Grump shrugs. "What can I say? They're terrifying."

Zenith turns its gaze toward you next, and you feel your stomach drop. "Now, it is your turn."

You swallow nervously, glancing at Matilda for reassurance. She gives you a small nod, but it does little to calm your nerves.

You take a deep breath and step forward, bracing yourself for whatever comes next.

Zenith raises its hand, and once again, the air around you shimmers. The strange, melodic hum fills your ears, and for a brief moment, everything goes still.

Then, without warning, the walls of the cavern begin to close in around you.

Your heart pounds in your chest as the space grows smaller and smaller, the walls pressing in from all sides. The air feels thick and heavy, making it hard to breathe. Your chest tightens, and a familiar sense of panic rises in your throat.

"Claustrophobia," you whisper to yourself. "This is just an illusion. It's not real."

But even as you say the words, the fear grips you tighter. The walls are so close now, you can barely move. Your pulse races, and your breath comes in short, shallow gasps.

"Stay calm," you tell yourself, trying to steady your breathing. "It's not real. You're not trapped."

The walls inch closer, and the air grows suffocating. You feel like you're being buried alive, your worst fear coming to life right before your eyes.

But then, you hear a voice. It's faint, barely a whisper, but it cuts through the panic.

"Accept it."

It's Zenith. The Keeper of the Nexus.

You close your eyes, forcing yourself to focus on your breathing. In and out. In and out. Slowly, you begin to relax, accepting the feeling of confinement rather than fighting it.

"It's not real," you remind yourself. "It can't hurt me."

And just like that, the walls stop closing in. The air clears, and the sensation of being trapped disappears. You open your eyes to find yourself standing in the cavern, unharmed.

Zenith nods once again. "You have faced your fear. You may proceed."

You let out a shaky breath, relieved that the ordeal is over.

Matilda steps forward, ready to face her own challenge, but before she can speak, Zenith raises a hand. "You will not be tested today. Your time will come."

Matilda looks confused but nods nonetheless. "I'll take that as a win."

Zenith turns to face the glowing Nexus once more. "You have proven yourselves worthy. The Nexus will guide you to your destination."

The pulsing light of the Nexus grows brighter, and you feel a strange warmth wash over you. The hum of the relaxing aura fills the air, and for a brief moment, you feel connected to something far greater than yourself.

And then, in a flash of light, everything goes dark.

Chapter 5: The Space Diner Debacle

Your eyes flicker open to a completely different setting. The hum of the relaxing aura fades away, replaced by the distant clatter of plates and the murmur of voices. You sit up quickly, your head spinning from the sudden change. You're no longer in the cavern, nor in front of the glowing Nexus. In fact, you're no longer in any kind of alien structure at all.

You're sitting in a diner. A space diner, to be exact.

The room is wide and brightly lit, with long rows of metallic booths, shiny chrome tables, and neon lights flashing menus in various alien languages. The air smells faintly of… something, but it's hard to say what. A mixture of burnt toast, engine grease, and some kind of floral scent that doesn't belong in a kitchen.

Matilda is sitting across from you, her eyes still shut, while Grump is already on his feet, inspecting the surroundings with childlike curiosity.

"Where are we?" you ask, blinking in confusion.

Grump grins, pointing toward a flashing neon sign above the counter. "Welcome to *Galax-Eat*, the finest space diner this side of the Milky Way!"

Matilda opens her eyes and glances around, a mix of annoyance and disbelief on her face. "A space diner? Are you serious?"

"Hey, I'm just as confused as you are," you mutter, standing up from the booth. "One minute we're talking to Zenith, and now we're... here?"

Grump's eyes light up as a robotic waiter rolls by, balancing a tray of alien food that glows an unsettling shade of green. "Who cares where we are? This place is amazing!"

You watch as the robot glides smoothly past your table, its mechanical limbs whirring softly as it delivers the food to a table of strange, insectoid aliens sitting nearby. The aliens buzz excitedly as the food is placed in front of them, their antennae twitching in anticipation.

Matilda folds her arms, glaring at Grump. "We're in the middle of trying to figure out how to get home, and all you can think about is food?"

Grump shrugs. "Hey, a guy's gotta eat. Besides, who knows how long we'll be here? Might as well take advantage of the free service."

"Free?" you ask skeptically, watching as another robotic waiter zooms past. "I'm not sure anything in a space diner is free."

As if on cue, a menu screen flickers to life at your table, displaying a list of "today's specials." You glance at it, your stomach growling in spite of the strange, unsettling names.

Galactic Goulash
Stellar Sausages
Nebula Nachos
Asteroid Pies (Warning: May Contain Actual Asteroids)

Matilda stares at the menu in horror. "What kind of place serves food that could *literally* kill you?"

Grump, however, is already tapping the screen eagerly. "I'll take one of everything!"

You can't help but laugh. "Grump, this is a bad idea. We don't even know what half of this stuff is."

Grump winks. "That's the fun part!"

Before you can stop him, he presses the *Order Now* button, and the robotic waiter wheels over to your table, its metal arms laden with plates of glowing, sizzling, and bubbling dishes. Each dish looks more alien and bizarre than the last.

Matilda watches in horror as the food is set in front of you. "I am *not* eating any of this."

Grump, on the other hand, grabs a fork and stabs into a plate of what looks like blue noodles topped with... some kind of shimmering sauce. "You don't know what you're missing, Matilda! This could be the best meal of your life."

Matilda leans back, crossing her arms. "Or the last."

Grump takes a bite, his eyes widening as the flavor hits his tongue. "Oh man, this is... *spicy*."

You and Matilda exchange glances, watching as Grump chews with increasing discomfort. His face slowly turns red, and beads of sweat form on his forehead. "Grump, are you okay?"

He waves a hand, trying to act casual. "Yeah... I'm fine... just... a little... hot."

"Your face is literally on fire," Matilda deadpans, pointing at the steam now rising from Grump's ears.

You reach over, grabbing a glass of water and sliding it toward him. "Maybe slow down?"

Grump grabs the glass, chugging the water in one gulp, but it doesn't seem to help. His face gets redder by the second, and you swear you see actual flames flickering behind his eyes.

Matilda rolls her eyes. "I warned you."

But Grump, ever the trooper, shakes it off. "No way! I'm not letting a little heat stop me!" He reaches for another bite of food, and you grab his hand, stopping him before he can dig in.

"Grump, seriously. Maybe it's time to call it quits before your head explodes."

Grump frowns but reluctantly sets his fork down. "Fine. But this food is *delicious*. It's just a bit... intense."

Matilda glares at the pile of strange dishes in front of you. "Intense is an understatement. How do we know any of this stuff is even edible?"

Before you can respond, the door to the diner swings open with a loud *clang*, and all the diners go silent. You glance over, your heart skipping a beat as a group of hulking figures enters the room.

They're massive—easily twice your size—with thick, leathery skin and glowing, yellow eyes. Their heads are adorned with horns, and they each carry a large, menacing-looking club strapped to their backs. The entire diner seems to hold its breath as they stomp toward the counter.

"Who are they?" you whisper, leaning toward Matilda.

"No idea," she replies, her voice low. "But I don't like the looks of them."

Grump, as usual, seems completely unfazed. "Maybe they're regulars! This is a diner, after all."

You watch as the hulking aliens approach the counter. The robotic waiter rolls up to them, but instead of placing an order, one of the aliens grabs the robot by the neck and lifts it into the air with one hand.

"Where's our food?" the alien growls, its voice deep and rumbling like thunder.

The robot's eyes flicker, its voice calm as ever. "Your order is being prepared. Please be patient."

The alien narrows its glowing yellow eyes. "We don't wait."

Without another word, the alien crushes the robot's neck, sending sparks flying as the machine crumples to the floor. The rest of the diner patrons watch in stunned silence as the alien drops the robot and turns to face the room.

Matilda grabs your arm, her voice barely above a whisper. "We need to get out of here."

Grump frowns. "I don't see the problem. They're just a little hangry."

You shake your head. "No, this is bad. If they're willing to smash a robot over a delayed order, imagine what they'll do to us."

The hulking alien at the counter scans the room, its eyes glowing as it looks for its next target. It locks eyes with your table, and you freeze, your heart pounding in your chest.

It starts toward you, its footsteps heavy and deliberate.

"Uh, guys?" you whisper. "We've got company."

Matilda's eyes widen, and Grump finally seems to catch on to the seriousness of the situation. "Oh... this might be a problem."

The alien reaches your table, looming over you like a mountain. Its glowing yellow eyes flick between the three of you, and for a moment, you wonder if you're about to become the diner's next victims.

But instead of attacking, the alien points at your plate of food. "Is that the Nebula Nachos?"

You blink, confused. "Uh... yeah, I think so?"

The alien grunts, crossing its massive arms. "They're supposed to come with extra space guacamole. I don't see any guacamole on your plate."

You glance down at the nachos, which are glowing faintly in the dim light. Sure enough, there's no sign of guacamole.

"I... I don't know what to tell you," you stammer. "We didn't order any guacamole."

The alien scowls, its eyes narrowing. "I hate it when they forget the guacamole."

Matilda leans forward, her voice cautious. "We could... ask the waiter to bring you some?"

The alien lets out a deep, rumbling sigh. "They never get the order right. Every time I come here, they forget something."

Grump, ever the diplomat, jumps in. "Well, you know, space diners aren't what they used to be! Back in the day, they had top-notch service. Now it's all robots and faulty systems."

The alien grunts in agreement. "Yeah, no kidding. Last time they forgot my asteroid fries. I was furious."

Matilda glances at you, bewildered. "Is this... actually happening?"

You shrug, equally confused. "I think it is."

Grump smiles at the alien. "Tell you what, why don't we split the nachos? We've got plenty, and it's always better with friends, right?"

The alien's expression softens slightly, and for a moment, you think Grump might have actually diffused the situation.

But then the alien's scowl returns. "No guacamole, no deal."

Before any of you can react, the alien grabs your plate of nachos and hurls it across the diner, sending it crashing into the wall. The other patrons gasp as the glowing nachos explode on impact, covering the walls in neon green sauce.

"Okay, that's it!" Matilda snaps, standing up from the table. "I've had enough of this!"

Grump grabs her arm. "Whoa, whoa! Let's not escalate things here."

But it's too late. The alien growls, its massive fists clenching as it looms over Matilda. "You got a problem, lady?"

Matilda glares up at the alien, her voice steady but firm. "Yeah, I do. You can't just go around throwing people's food. That's rude."

The alien's eyes blaze with anger, and for a brief moment, you think a fight is about to break out. But then, to your surprise, the alien lets out a loud, rumbling laugh.

"You've got guts," it says, slapping Matilda on the back hard enough to nearly knock her over. "I like that."

Matilda, clearly taken aback, stumbles slightly before regaining her composure. "Uh... thanks?"

The alien nods, stepping back. "Next time, I'll buy the nachos. With extra guacamole."

With that, the hulking alien turns and stomps back to the counter, leaving the three of you standing there in stunned silence.

Grump lets out a long breath, wiping sweat from his forehead. "Well, that was... something."

You collapse back into your seat, your heart still racing. "I can't believe that worked."

Matilda shakes her head, sitting back down as well. "I can't believe this is our life now."

Grump, ever the optimist, grins as he grabs a piece of the remaining alien food from the table. "Hey, look on the bright side—at least we didn't get pulverized!"

Matilda glares at him. "You really need to stop finding the bright side of every near-death experience."

But despite the tension, you can't help but laugh. As absurd as it all is, this is the Galaxy of Comedy, after all—and sometimes, all you can do is laugh.

Chapter 6: Space Hitchhiker's Dilemma

The tension from the space diner encounter has barely worn off when you find yourselves back in the thick of it—on the move once again, wandering through the strange new galaxy in search of... well, anything that could help you get back home. After the near-death experience with the hulking alien and his guacamole dilemma, you're hoping for a little less excitement and a lot more clarity on what exactly you're supposed to do next.

"Could've gone worse," Grump says cheerfully, as if you all didn't nearly end up as mashed space potatoes back at the diner. "At least we know space diners aren't all fun and games. Or good customer service."

Matilda rolls her eyes, still clearly annoyed by the whole ordeal. "I'd say the fact that we survived a food fight with an angry alien means we should be a little more cautious going forward. This isn't some comic book."

You glance around, taking in your surroundings. The landscape is alien, of course, with jagged purple rocks jutting up from the ground, glowing in the eerie light of the galaxy's twin suns. The ground crunches beneath your feet, feeling oddly like broken glass, though it doesn't cut you. The sky is a swirl of green and pink clouds, and somewhere in the distance, you can hear a faint hum, like the whirring of an engine.

"So where do we go from here?" you ask, trying to keep your tone casual despite the unease gnawing at your stomach. "We've survived robot attacks, food fights, and some weird consciousness test, but we're still no closer to finding our way home."

"Relax," Grump says, tapping a small handheld device he's been fiddling with for the last few minutes. "This little gadget should help us locate a nearby portal. Just give it a second to calibrate."

Matilda gives him a skeptical look. "Are you sure that thing isn't just going to explode in your hands?"

Grump shrugs. "Probably not. But hey, no risk, no reward, right?"

You sigh, already bracing yourself for the inevitable malfunction when a strange sound interrupts your thoughts. It's faint at first, barely audible over the hum of the alien environment, but it quickly grows louder. It's a mechanical whirring sound, accompanied by the unmistakable roar of an engine.

You stop walking, holding up a hand to signal the others. "Wait. Do you hear that?"

Matilda and Grump freeze, their expressions shifting to curiosity. The sound is getting closer, and before you can fully process what's happening, a sleek, silver spacecraft appears in the distance, zooming toward you at breakneck speed.

"Uh... should we be worried?" Matilda asks, her voice tense.

Grump squints at the rapidly approaching ship. "Nah, it's probably just a friendly passerby. You know, the intergalactic equivalent of a taxi."

Matilda raises an eyebrow. "Somehow, I doubt that."

As the ship draws closer, you can see more details—its smooth, metallic surface glinting in the light of the twin suns, and the bright neon lights flashing across its sides. It looks like something straight out of an old sci-fi movie, complete with glowing thrusters and an unnecessarily flashy design.

Just when you're about to suggest ducking for cover, the ship slows down, hovering in the air a few feet above you. A side door slides open with a soft *whoosh*, and a figure steps out onto the extended ramp.

You can't quite believe your eyes. The figure is tall, wearing what can only be described as a cross between a spacesuit and a Hawaiian shirt. His hair is wild, sticking out in all directions, and he's wearing sunglasses that seem far too casual for deep-space travel. He grins at you, flashing a set of unnaturally white teeth, and waves enthusiastically.

"Well, well, well!" the man calls out, his voice dripping with confidence. "What do we have here? A trio of space travelers in need of some assistance, perhaps?"

Grump's face lights up. "Told you! Friendly passerby."

Matilda crosses her arms, her expression unreadable. "He looks... questionable."

You can't help but agree. There's something off about this guy—something a little too polished, too rehearsed, like he's trying too hard to fit the role of a charming space traveler. Still, you don't have many options, and you're not in a position to turn down help.

The man saunters down the ramp, his sunglasses reflecting the twin suns as he approaches. "Name's Captain Dash, best pilot in the galaxy! Need a lift?"

You exchange glances with Matilda and Grump, unsure of how to respond. This Captain Dash seems way too good to be true, but at the same time, you could really use a break from wandering aimlessly through alien landscapes.

"What's the catch?" Matilda asks, ever the cautious one.

Captain Dash laughs, the sound almost too smooth to be genuine. "No catch, sweetheart! I'm just out here, cruising the stars, looking for adventure. Saw you guys from a distance and figured you could use a ride. No strings attached!"

Grump is already nodding eagerly. "Sounds like a great deal to me! I say we take him up on it."

Matilda glares at him. "You trust this guy?"

Grump shrugs. "Why not? He seems harmless enough. Besides, what's the worst that could happen?"

You open your mouth to point out that "the worst that could happen" usually involves explosions, kidnappings, or intergalactic disasters, but before you can voice your concerns, Captain Dash steps forward, clapping a hand on your shoulder.

"Come on, what do you say?" he asks, his grin widening. "Hop aboard the *Starduster*, and I'll get you where you need to go. No charge, no trouble."

You glance at Matilda, who's still clearly skeptical, but you can see that even she's considering the offer. After all, you're stuck in the middle of an alien wasteland with no other options in sight.

Finally, you nod. "Okay. We'll take the ride."

Captain Dash's grin grows even wider, and he gestures toward the ship. "Excellent choice! You won't regret it, I promise."

As the three of you make your way toward the *Starduster*, you can't shake the feeling that something is off. Captain Dash's easy charm and too-perfect smile seem designed to put you at ease, but your instincts are telling you to stay on guard.

The interior of the ship is just as flashy as the exterior. Bright neon lights line the walls, and the control panels are covered in holographic displays that flash and flicker with dizzying speed. The seats are upholstered in what looks like shimmering purple leather, and the whole place feels more like a space nightclub than a functional spacecraft.

Grump, of course, is already in awe. "This place is incredible! Look at the tech! This ship must be state-of-the-art!"

Captain Dash plops down in the pilot's seat, kicking his feet up on the dashboard. "State-of-the-art, alright. The *Starduster* is the fastest, smoothest ride in the galaxy. You're in good hands."

Matilda, however, remains unconvinced. "I'm still waiting for the catch."

Dash winks at her. "No catch! Just a smooth ride to wherever you're headed."

You settle into one of the plush seats, trying to relax despite the nagging feeling in your gut. Captain Dash seems friendly enough, but something about his over-the-top confidence makes you uneasy. Still, you have no better options at the moment, and you're not about to turn down a free ride.

"So, where are you guys headed?" Dash asks, flipping switches on the control panel with casual ease.

"We're trying to find a way back to our own galaxy," you explain, leaning forward slightly. "We got here by accident—activated a portal that sent us to this place."

Dash raises an eyebrow. "A portal, huh? Sounds like you've had quite the adventure."

"That's one way to put it," Matilda mutters under her breath.

Grump, as usual, is much more enthusiastic. "Yeah! We've been through all kinds of crazy stuff—robots, alien diners, you name it! But now we just need to get home."

Dash nods, tapping the control panel. "Well, lucky for you, I know just the shortcut. It's a bit off the beaten path, but it'll get you where you need to go in no time."

You glance at Matilda, who gives you a look that says, *I told you there was a catch.*

"A shortcut?" you ask, trying to keep your voice steady. "How do we know it's safe?"

Dash laughs, waving a hand dismissively. "Safe? Kid, nothing in this galaxy is truly safe. But trust me, I've been flying this route for years. I know all the tricks and turns. Just sit back and enjoy the ride."

The ship's engines roar to life, and the *Starduster* lifts off the ground with a smooth, almost effortless motion. You watch as the alien landscape below shrinks away, replaced by the swirling colors of the galaxy as the ship accelerates into space.

At first, everything seems fine. The ship hums quietly, and Captain Dash hums along with it, clearly in his element. But after a few minutes, you start to notice something odd.

The stars outside the window seem to be moving... wrong.

Instead of streaking past like they normally do when a ship enters hyperspace, the stars seem to swirl and twist, bending in ways that make your head spin. The ship jerks slightly, and you feel your stomach lurch as gravity seems to shift beneath you.

"Uh... Captain Dash?" you say, gripping the armrests of your seat. "Are we supposed to be... spinning?"

Dash's grin doesn't falter. "Oh, don't worry about that. We're just hitting a little turbulence. Completely normal for this route."

Matilda narrows her eyes. "Turbulence in space?"

Grump, still oblivious, is too busy admiring the ship's control systems to notice anything unusual. "Wow, this tech is amazing! I've never seen a ship with this kind of interface before!"

But you're starting to feel more than a little queasy. The ship continues to jerk and spin, and the stars outside warp and bend in ways that defy logic.

"Okay, this is not normal," you say, your voice rising with panic. "What's happening?"

Dash finally drops his carefree act, his grin fading as he grips the controls tightly. "Alright, I'll level with you—this shortcut is a little... unconventional."

Matilda groans. "Unconventional? What does that even mean?"

Dash grimaces. "It means we're flying through a spatial anomaly. It messes with gravity, time, and space. But don't worry, I've done this a thousand times! We'll be fine."

"Spatial anomaly?!" you shout, your heart pounding. "Are you insane?"

Dash laughs nervously. "Relax, I've got this. I'm the best pilot in the galaxy, remember?"

But as the ship lurches violently again, you're not so sure.

Chapter 7: The Phobia Showdown

The *Starduster* lurches violently as you hold on for dear life, the ship spiraling through the spatial anomaly with increasing speed. The stars outside the window twist and warp into unrecognizable shapes, and you feel your stomach flip as gravity shifts unpredictably. Captain Dash is gripping the controls, his carefree grin replaced by a tense frown.

"This... is not fun!" Matilda shouts over the roar of the ship's engines, her hands clutching the armrests of her seat.

Grump, ever the optimist, is still tapping away at the ship's control panel. "It's fine! We're just bending the fabric of space and time a little bit. Happens all the time!"

Matilda shoots him a withering glare. "That is not comforting!"

You can barely hold onto your seat as the ship jerks again, this time with enough force to knock you sideways. "Captain Dash! Are we going to make it through this anomaly or not?"

Dash glances over his shoulder, his face pale but still managing to maintain an air of overconfidence. "Oh, yeah, totally. Just a few more bumps, and we'll be through it in no time!"

But the "bumps" aren't letting up. If anything, they're getting worse.

The ship spins wildly as the gravitational forces of the anomaly pull at it from every direction. You try to steady yourself, gripping the edges of your seat as tightly as you can, but you're starting to lose your sense of up and down. Everything inside the ship feels like it's being turned upside down, and the nauseating sensation makes your head spin.

Suddenly, a loud *crack* echoes through the ship, followed by a series of beeping alarms.

"What now?" you groan, struggling to keep your eyes open as the ship continues to pitch and yaw uncontrollably.

Captain Dash frowns at the flashing lights on his console. "Looks like we've got some damage to the stabilizers. Nothing major! We'll just... have to land."

"Land?" Matilda's voice rises in pitch. "On what? We're in the middle of a spatial anomaly!"

Dash doesn't answer right away, his fingers flying over the control panel as he punches in coordinates. "Hold on tight, folks. We're about to exit the anomaly. We just need to find a safe place to touch down."

As if on cue, the swirling, chaotic stars outside begin to stabilize, the colors fading back into the familiar blackness of space. The ship's violent shaking eases up, though the alarms continue to blare, and you can feel the subtle tremors beneath your feet.

"We're almost out," Dash says, his voice tight with concentration. "Hang on just a little longer."

You glance out the window and see a planet looming ahead—its surface covered in vast mountain ranges and towering cliffs. It looks inhospitable, to say the least, but given the state of the ship, you don't have much of a choice.

"That doesn't look like a safe landing zone," you say, pointing to the jagged peaks below.

"Beggars can't be choosers," Dash replies with a strained smile. "I'll find us a smooth patch of ground... somewhere."

The ship descends rapidly, and the closer you get to the planet's surface, the more your anxiety spikes. The mountains below seem to stretch endlessly, their sharp ridges casting long shadows across the desolate landscape. There's no sign of civilization—just barren rock and steep cliffs that drop off into dizzying abysses.

Matilda is gripping her seat, her knuckles white. "We're not really landing there, are we?"

Grump, oblivious as usual, is still fiddling with the control panel. "Relax, it'll be fine. Dash is a professional."

You're not so sure about that.

The ship jerks again as it enters the planet's atmosphere, the heat from reentry causing the hull to rattle. Captain Dash adjusts the controls, his eyes scanning the landscape for a suitable landing spot.

"There!" he says, pointing to a narrow plateau nestled between two towering cliffs. "I can set us down there."

You watch as the *Starduster* heads toward the plateau, its engines straining as Dash maneuvers the ship between the jagged peaks. The landing isn't exactly smooth—the ship lurches and tilts as it touches down, the sound of scraping metal filling the cabin—but you manage to land in one piece.

Barely.

The ship finally comes to a stop, the alarms quieting down as the engines power off. You let out a shaky breath, thankful to be back on solid ground—even if that solid ground is on a desolate, cliff-filled planet in the middle of nowhere.

"Well, that wasn't so bad," Grump says, unbuckling his seatbelt with a grin.

Matilda shoots him a look that could freeze water. "I swear, Grump, if you say one more thing about how 'fine' everything is, I'm going to—"

But before she can finish, the ship's door opens with a soft *whoosh*, and you're hit by a blast of cold air. You shiver, stepping out of the ship and onto the rocky surface of the plateau. The wind howls around you, and you can see dark storm clouds gathering on the horizon.

"This place is giving me the creeps," you mutter, scanning the jagged landscape.

Matilda follows close behind, her face pale as she stares at the steep cliffs surrounding the plateau. "I don't like this. It's too… high."

You glance at her, noticing the tight grip she has on the side of the ship. Matilda's phobia of heights is well-known by now, but this situation seems to be pushing her to the limit.

"We're safe as long as we stay away from the edges," you reassure her, though you're not entirely convinced of that yourself.

Captain Dash steps out of the ship, stretching his arms and flashing you a confident smile. "Not bad, right? We made it out of the anomaly, and now we just need to fix up the ship. Piece of cake!"

Matilda doesn't look convinced. She takes a few steps away from the ship, her eyes locked on the distant cliffs. "I can't… I can't stay here."

You frown, stepping closer to her. "Matilda, it's okay. We're not going anywhere near the edge. We'll stay here until the ship is fixed."

But Matilda shakes her head, her breathing quickening. "No. It's too high. I can feel it... the drop... I can't—"

Before you can react, Matilda suddenly stumbles, her foot slipping on the rocky ground. You reach out to catch her, but she pulls away, panic in her eyes.

And then, in one horrifying moment, she loses her balance completely and tumbles toward the edge of the plateau.

"Matilda!" you shout, rushing forward.

Grump, moving faster than you've ever seen him move, dives toward her, grabbing her arm just as she reaches the precipice. The two of them teeter on the edge for a moment, and your heart skips a beat as you imagine them both going over.

But Grump manages to pull her back just in time, and the two of them collapse onto the ground, breathing heavily.

"Are you okay?" you ask, your heart still racing.

Matilda nods shakily, but her eyes are wide with fear. "I... I almost..."

"You're fine," Grump says, helping her to her feet. "You're not going anywhere near that edge again."

Matilda takes a deep breath, trying to steady herself, but you can see that the fear is still there—raw and overwhelming.

"I can't... I can't stay here," she whispers again. "I need to get off this planet."

You glance at Captain Dash, who is inspecting the ship's exterior. "How long until we can leave?"

Dash rubs the back of his neck, looking a little sheepish. "Well, that's the thing... the stabilizers are pretty shot. I'll need a few hours to patch them up, assuming I can find the right materials."

Matilda's face pales even further. "Hours? We don't have hours!"

You place a hand on her shoulder, trying to calm her. "We'll be fine, Matilda. Just stay inside the ship. You don't have to be out here."

But she shakes her head, clearly not hearing you. "I can't. I can't stay. It's too much. I'm going to—"

"Matilda," you say softly, crouching down in front of her. "Listen to me. You're okay. You're not going to fall. We're all right here with you. Just focus on your breathing, okay?"

Grump, standing nearby, looks genuinely concerned. "We'll figure something out. There's gotta be a way to help her."

Captain Dash walks over, arms crossed. "Phobia of heights, huh? Tough break. But hey, facing your fear is the best way to beat it, right?"

Matilda glares at him. "I don't need a lecture."

"No lecture," Dash says, holding up his hands. "Just a little advice from someone who's seen it all. Trust me, the only way to get over that fear is to take control of it."

You glance at Dash, skeptical. "And how do you suggest we do that?"

84

Dash grins. "Simple. You face it head-on."

Matilda stares at him, horrified. "You want me to go near the edge again? Are you out of your mind?"

Dash shrugs. "Maybe. But what if you could beat this thing? What if, by the time we leave this planet, heights don't scare you anymore?"

Matilda looks torn between terror and the faintest flicker of hope. "How?"

Dash points to the edge of the plateau. "You're not going to jump, obviously. But you need to get closer. Take small steps. Get used to it. I'll be right there with you."

Grump raises an eyebrow. "I don't know if this is the best idea."

Matilda hesitates, but then, with a deep breath, she nods. "I'll... try."

You watch, unsure if this is bravery or madness, as Matilda takes slow, shaky steps toward the edge of the plateau. Dash walks alongside her, talking softly, guiding her movements.

As they approach the edge, Matilda's breathing quickens again, but she doesn't stop. Step by step, she gets closer, until finally, she's standing just a few feet from the drop.

She closes her eyes, her fists clenched tightly at her sides. "I can do this," she whispers. "I can do this."

You hold your breath, watching in awe as Matilda takes one final step forward, her toes just inches from the edge. For a moment, the wind howls around her, and you can see the fear etched into her features.

But then, slowly, she opens her eyes.

And she smiles.

Chapter 8: The Curing Moment

Matilda stands at the edge of the plateau, the wind whipping through her hair, her eyes wide but filled with determination. You watch in stunned silence as she gazes out over the endless drop below, her fear still palpable but no longer paralyzing.

Grump, who had been holding his breath, lets out a soft cheer. "She's doing it! She's actually doing it!"

Captain Dash, standing a few steps behind Matilda, grins proudly. "Told you. Facing your fear is the only way to beat it."

Matilda, her feet rooted to the spot, takes another slow, deep breath. She's trembling slightly, but you can see the progress. Her phobia isn't gone—fear that deep never disappears in an instant—but something has shifted. She's no longer running from it.

You step forward cautiously, not wanting to startle her. "Matilda... how do you feel?"

She doesn't answer right away, her gaze still fixed on the horizon. Finally, after what feels like an eternity, she speaks. "I... I feel scared," she admits, her voice soft. "But I also feel... in control."

Captain Dash steps up beside her, nodding approvingly. "That's it. Control. It's all about taking back control. You're stronger than you think."

Matilda lets out a shaky laugh, glancing over at him. "Maybe you're not as reckless as you seem."

Dash chuckles. "Oh, I'm definitely reckless. But I'm also right about this."

You can't help but smile as you watch Matilda take another deep breath, her shoulders relaxing just a little. For the first time since you've known her, she looks like she's not fighting against her fear—but working with it. It's a huge step, and you're proud of her.

Grump claps his hands together. "Well, now that Matilda's cured, what's next? We still have a ship to fix, right?"

Captain Dash nods, pulling out a small toolkit from his belt. "Right you are, Grump. Stabilizers are busted, but nothing I can't patch up. Shouldn't take more than an hour or two, and then we'll be good to go."

Matilda takes one last look at the edge of the plateau before turning back to the group. "Let's get out of here. I think I've faced enough of my fears for one day."

You all head back toward the ship, the tension that had been hanging over the group finally starting to lift. Dash kneels beside the stabilizers, pulling off a few panels and inspecting the damage. Grump immediately joins him, eager to help with the repairs.

"Okay," Dash says, pointing to a few sparking wires. "I need you to rewire that, and I'll work on patching this panel up. We need to recalibrate the flux dampeners and balance the gravitational modulator."

Grump grins, already elbow-deep in wires. "Oh, this is gonna be fun."

Matilda, still looking a little shaky from her recent ordeal, leans against the ship's hull, her arms crossed. "I hope you know what you're doing, Dash. I don't want to end up in another anomaly."

Dash laughs, tossing her a wink. "Relax. We'll be back in regular space in no time. And don't worry, no more shortcuts. I promise."

You sit down next to Matilda, feeling a wave of exhaustion wash over you. It's been a long journey filled with bizarre encounters, close calls, and more chaos than you could have ever predicted. But somehow, through it all, you've managed to keep it together—and now, you're finally on your way back.

Matilda glances over at you, her expression softening. "Thanks."

"For what?" you ask, surprised.

"For... everything," she says, her voice quieter than usual. "I don't know if I could have done this without you."

You smile, shrugging. "We're a team. We've all got each other's backs."

She nods, looking thoughtful. "Still… I appreciate it."

The two of you sit in comfortable silence as Dash and Grump work on the ship. Every now and then, you hear the clang of tools or the crackle of sparks, but otherwise, it's peaceful. The storm clouds that had been gathering on the horizon seem to be dissipating, and the sky above the plateau is clear and bright.

Finally, after what feels like an eternity, Dash straightens up, wiping his hands on a rag. "Alright, folks! She's all patched up and ready to fly!"

Grump steps back, admiring their handiwork. "I gotta hand it to you, Dash. You really know your way around a ship."

Dash grins. "Told you, I'm the best pilot in the galaxy."

Matilda gives him a skeptical look. "Let's see if you can live up to that claim."

You all board the *Starduster* once again, and as the engines hum to life, you feel a sense of relief wash over you. It's time to leave this planet behind and get back on track—back to familiar territory.

The ship lifts off the ground smoothly this time, and within minutes, you're soaring above the jagged cliffs and mountain ranges. The stars stretch out before you, vast and endless, and you can't help but feel a little awe-struck by the beauty of the galaxy.

Dash sits at the controls, whistling cheerfully as he adjusts the ship's course. "Next stop, the nearest spaceport. I'll get you folks on your way back home in no time."

You lean back in your seat, finally allowing yourself to relax. The journey has been wild, to say the least, but you're almost through it. Soon, you'll be back in familiar space, and hopefully back to your regular, less chaotic life.

Or at least, that's the plan.

Just as you're about to close your eyes, a loud beeping sound echoes through the cockpit.

"Oh, come on!" Matilda groans, sitting up straight. "Now what?"

Dash frowns, glancing at the control panel. "We've got company."

You glance out the window and see a small fleet of ships approaching fast, their sleek, black hulls glinting menacingly in the starlight. They're clearly not friendly.

Grump squints at the approaching ships. "Who are they?"

Dash's expression turns grim. "Pirates."

"Pirates?" you repeat, your heart sinking.

"Yup," Dash says, flipping switches and pulling the ship into a tight turn. "They've been trailing me for a while now. I was hoping to shake them, but it looks like they finally caught up."

Matilda grips her seat, her eyes wide with alarm. "You've got to be kidding me."

Dash doesn't answer. He's too focused on steering the ship as it weaves and dodges the incoming pirate vessels. The *Starduster* hums with power as it accelerates, but the pirates are fast, and they're gaining on you.

Grump looks worried for the first time all day. "Any chance we can outrun them?"

Dash grits his teeth. "I'm working on it. Just hold on tight!"

The ship jolts as a blast from one of the pirate ships skims past the hull, and you hear the alarms blare once again.

"This just keeps getting better," you mutter, gripping your seat.

Matilda shoots you a look. "We should have known there'd be more trouble."

Dash pulls the ship into a steep dive, dodging another barrage of laser fire. "We've got to lose them in the asteroid field ahead. It's risky, but it's our only shot!"

You glance at the asteroid field on the horizon, a swirling mass of rocks and debris that looks more dangerous than the pirates chasing you. But right now, it seems like your best option.

Dash steers the *Starduster* into the asteroid field, weaving between the massive rocks with surprising precision. The pirate ships follow, their weapons firing wildly, but the asteroids provide cover.

"We're not out of the woods yet," Dash says, his voice tight with concentration. "But if we can get through this field, they'll back off. Pirates don't like taking risks."

The ship jolts again as it scrapes past a massive asteroid, but Dash keeps it steady, navigating through the treacherous terrain with ease. The pirate ships fall back, their weapons struggling to hit their mark in the chaos of the asteroid field.

Finally, after what feels like an eternity, the pirate ships pull away, disappearing into the distance. The alarms on the *Starduster* go quiet, and the ship returns to its smooth, steady flight.

Dash lets out a breath he didn't know he was holding. "Looks like we made it."

Matilda, still gripping her seat, glares at him. "You didn't mention anything about pirates when we got on this ship."

Dash grins sheepishly. "Didn't think it'd be a problem. Guess I was wrong."

You chuckle, shaking your head. "Just another day in the Galaxy of Comedy, huh?"

Grump laughs, slapping Dash on the back. "I have to admit, that was pretty impressive."

Dash flashes his usual confident grin. "Told you I'm the best pilot in the galaxy."

Matilda rolls her eyes, but there's a hint of amusement in her expression. "Let's just get to the spaceport without any more surprises, okay?"

Dash salutes her. "Aye, aye, Captain."

As the *Starduster* speeds away from the asteroid field, the crew finally relaxes, thinking they've escaped the danger. Captain Dash hums cheerfully at the controls, and Grump is already tinkering with a new gadget he found in the ship. Matilda leans back, still recovering from her victory over her fear of heights.

But then, the radar screen on the control panel begins to blink—faint at first, then more urgently. Dash frowns and leans forward, tapping the screen.

"What now?" you ask, feeling the tension creeping back.

Dash narrows his eyes, staring at the flashing signal on the radar. "We've got a ship approaching. Fast."

"Pirates again?" Matilda groans.

"No..." Dash's voice trails off, his usual swagger gone. "This is something different."

The radar beeps faster, and just as you glance out the window, you see it—a massive, sleek spaceship, ten times the size of the *Starduster*, emerging from hyperspace directly in your path. The ship's metallic hull glistens in the starlight, and its glowing insignia—a strange, unfamiliar symbol—casts an ominous shadow over your vessel.

Dash swallows hard, his hands gripping the controls tightly. "That's... not good."

You lean forward, dread creeping into your voice. "Who is it?"

Dash hesitates for a moment, his face pale. "It's the Federation... and they're not here to negotiate."

Before you can process his words, the ship's lights flicker, and the communication console crackles to life. A cold, authoritative voice echoes through the cockpit.

"*Starduster*, this is the Galactic Federation. You are ordered to surrender immediately, or be destroyed."

As the ship glides smoothly through space, you can't help but smile. The journey has been wild, unpredictable, and full of mishaps, but somehow, you've made it through.

And as you sit back, watching the stars stretch out before you, you can't help but wonder what new adventures await in the next chapter of the Galaxy of Comedy.

More from the Author

Discover more exciting adventures and life-enhancing tips at chooseyourquest.net. Dive into a world of interactive fantasy storytelling designed to boost your mental resilience and well-being. Explore our collection of books and embark on journeys that entertain, educate, and empower you.

- Choose Your Quest to Mental Resilience
- Choose Your Quest to Survive the Island
- Choose Your Quest to Dream World
- Choose Your Quest to Win the Tournament, Part 1
- Choose Your Quest to Win the Tournament, Part 2

    If you enjoy my books, I would greatly appreciate your constructive review on Amazon and Goodreads. Your feedback helps other readers interested in mental health support and adventure discover these books.

Printed in Great Britain
by Amazon